I0760085

Wild about moms.

PHILIP BUNTING

It's not only humans who can be great moms. There are plenty of marvelous mothers out in the wild, too! Many wild moms go to great lengths to give their children the best chance of growing up healthy, smart and strong.

Some moms don't get much sleep.

Bottlenose dolphin.

Like some of their human cousins, bottlenose calves are terrible sleepers. Newborn dolphins don't sleep a wink for the first month of their lives, so neither do their poor moms.

Some moms have a spring in their step.

Kangaroo.
Kangaroo moms keep their babies in their pouches for around six months. Once they have grown, the joeys hop out to explore the great wide land beyond. But if they are startled, even baby roos that can bounce around on their own won't hesitate to spring back into the snug safety of the pouch!

Some moms know the way back home.

Green sea turtle.
When they're ready to lay their eggs, green sea turtle mothers return to the same beach where they once hatched. These turtles can lay hundreds of eggs in one nesting season and, in time, those baby turtles will return to the same beach to lay their own eggs.

Some moms like to decorate.

Knobbed hornbill.

Female knobbed hornbills build their nests inside large tree hollows. To stop sneaky snakes and other ravenous reptiles from slipping in to munch her eggs, the mother hornbill blocks off the entrance to her nest almost entirely, sealing herself inside with her eggs. She uses a very special building material for this – her own poop!

Some moms call in babysitters.

Giraffe.

After a few gentle nudges from mom, baby giraffes can typically walk within an hour or so of being born. However, newborns are not very quick on their feet. So while she goes off to gather lunch, a giraffe mom will leave her baby in the trusted care of other female giraffe babysitters.

Some moms build their kids a den.

Polar bear.

Mama polar bears give birth in the middle of the icy Arctic winter. So, very sensibly, they dig dens to keep their cubs cozy, safe and warm throughout those cold months. Once spring arrives, the cubs venture outside the den for the very first time, and the mama bears teach them to hunt.

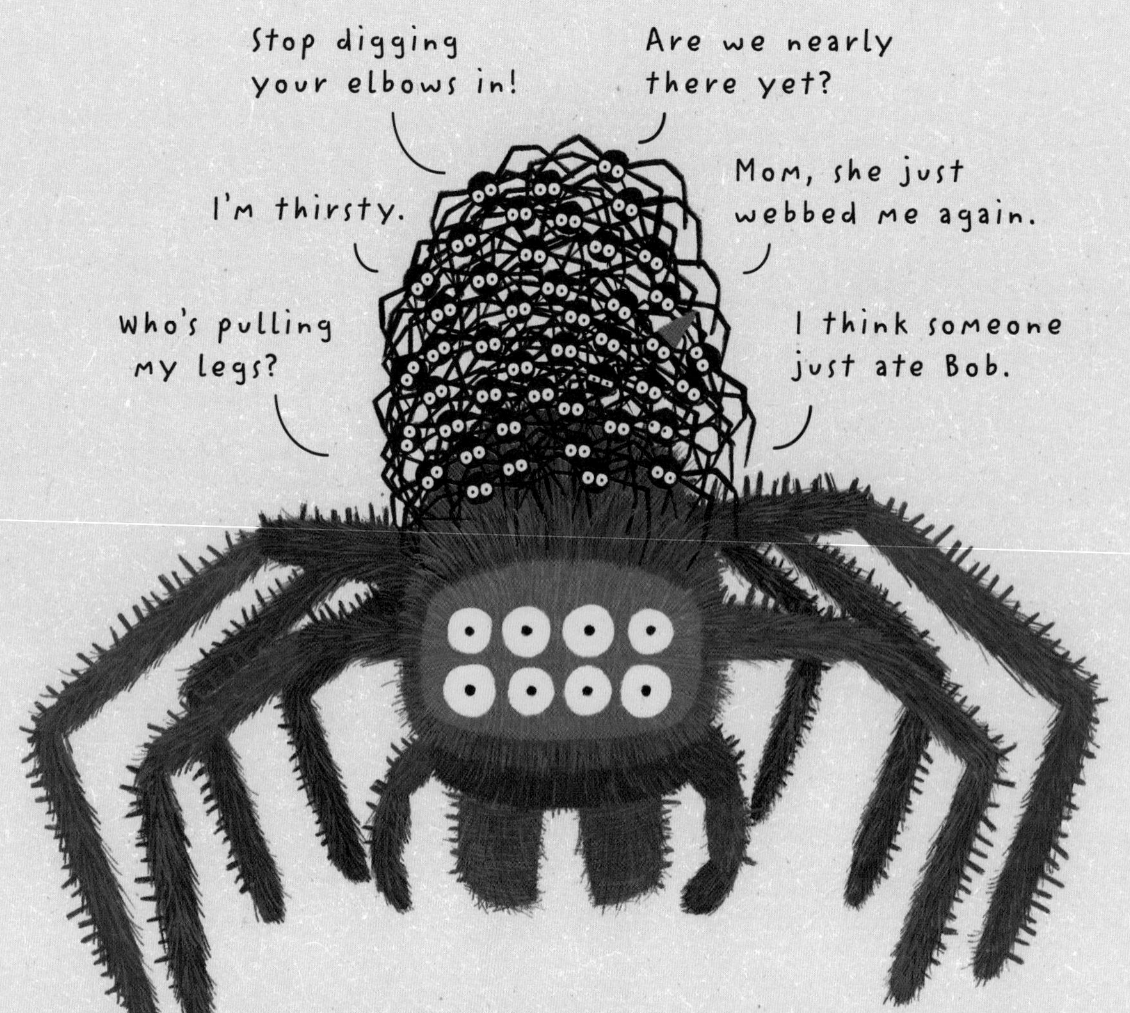

Some moms lug a lot of little ones.

Wolf spider.

Most spiders lay their eggs around their web, but not the wolf spider. This hairy mama carries her eggs around in a silky sack until they hatch. Once the incy wincy spiders are born, they all hitch a ride on their mom's bristly back until they're ready to make their own way in the world.

Some moms serve up special snacks.

Koala.

Koalas survive on a unique diet of highly toxic eucalyptus leaves. Luckily, their digestive system is equipped with a very special bacteria to help them digest these deadly greens. But koala joeys aren't born with these superpowers, so their moms serve up a special snack to help get their tummies ready to digest leaves. This little treat has just one ingredient ... their mama's scat.

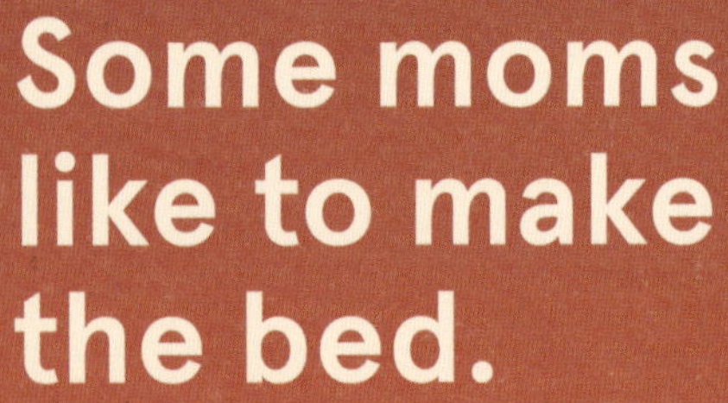

Some moms like to make the bed.

Orangutan.

Orangutan moms keep their babies by their sides for up to seven years, and during this time the two form a particularly close bond. Orangutans use branches and fresh leaves to make cozy beds for themselves and their little ones, and they make a brand-new nest every single night.

Some moms keep their kids afloat.

Sea otter.

Once a sea otter pup is born, its loving mother spends hours grooming it. This process gives the pup a lovely fluffy coat, which – as well as looking rather cute – traps heaps of tiny air bubbles within the pup's fur. The pup's newly fluffy coat acts as both a wetsuit and a lifejacket, helping to keep the pup warm and afloat!

Some moms know it takes a village.

African elephant.

African elephants are born completely blind, so they rely on their mother for guidance. These big, sightless babies are born into a matriarchal group of female elephants, so it isn't just their mother looking out for them – the entire group lends a trunk or tail to help raise the babies. Young elephants seem pretty happy with this arrangement, as they tend to stick with their mother and the rest of the herd until late into their teenage years.

Burp.
Some moms can get a bit peckish.
Giant Pacific octopus.
While hatching their eggs, octomoms are so committed to the wellbeing of their brood that they won't leave the nest – not even to feed themselves. It can take months for the eggs to hatch, and during this time octopus moms have been known to get so hungry that they eat their own arms! So what do you call an octopus with seven arms? A septopus? Nope – a very dedicated mom.

Some moms give their pups seal training.

Weddell seal.

These big mamas give their pups the best possible coaching, guiding them each step of the way as they grow. Weddell seal moms teach their pups to swim, hunt, navigate and thrive in the icy-cold Antarctic waters that they call home.

Some moms give a snappy ride.

Alligator.

Alligators hatch their eggs in wonderful waterside nests made from twigs and grass. Once the baby gators hatch, their loving mother gently carries them in her mouth – or on top of her head – until they are ready to swim.

Onward!

Some moms go a long, long way.

Humpback whale.
To give their babies the warmest possible welcome to the world, humpback whale moms leave the cold polar waters and undertake huge journeys so that their calves can be born in warm, tropical waters. Each humpback mom closely guides and protects their baby for at least a year before the calf makes its way into the wide blue yonder.

Some moms make great teachers.

Cheetah.

Cheetah moms don't take shortcuts. These wild moms spend around two years intensively teaching their cubs to play, hunt and be dotty. Once the cubs have graduated from their mom's care, the litter sticks together for up to a year.

What does your mom do for you?

Cheetah.
Acinonyx jubatus.
☑ Mammal
☑ Africa
☑ 128km/h
☑ Great mum

FOR MILLY

XX

While they each express it in their own particular way, the force that moves these wild moms is universal.

Little Hare
an imprint of Hardie Grant Children's Publishing
Wurundjeri Country
Level 11, 36 Wellington Street
Collingwood Victoria 3066
Melbourne | Sydney | San Francisco

hardiegrant.com/childrens

ISBN: 9781761217012

First published in Australia in 2021
This edition published in 2026

Printed and bound in HeShan China, November 2025
by LEO Paper Products LTD.

The paper this book is printed on is from FSC® certified forests and other controlled sources. FSC® promotes environmentally responsible, socially beneficial and economically viable management of the world's forests.

5 4 3 2 1

Hardie Grant acknowledges the Traditional Owners of the Country on which we work, the Wurundjeri People of the Kulin Nation and the Gadigal People of the Eora Nation, and recognises their continuing connection to the land, waters and culture. We pay our respects to their Elders past and present.